NATIONAL GEOGRAPHIC

Living It Up
in Space

PIONEER EDITION

By Nancy Finton

CONTENTS

LIVING IT UP IN SPACE

What is it like to live 220 miles above Earth? We asked a space station commander!

BY NANCY FINTO

Right now, people are zooming through space. They speed along at 17,000 miles per hour. Who would do that? **Astronauts!** They are people who travel into space.

Today, astronauts are working on the **International Space Station,** or ISS. It is a huge spacecraft. It is the astronauts' home away from Earth.

Living in space is not easy. It gets super hot and cold. There is no air. But that is not all that is different.

Up in Space

In space, everything floats around. Why? There is not much **gravity.**

On Earth, gravity is what keeps your feet on the ground. In space, there is less gravity. So people do not stand. They float!

Bill Shepherd was the first commander of the ISS. He thinks floating in space is fun. Shepherd says, "It is like moving in a swimming pool. Only you are even lighter!"

Dressed for Success.
Bill Shepherd did not need a space suit inside the ISS. But no astronaut can work outside the station without one.

Light Snack.
Tuna can act a little fishy in space. This astronaut's tuna is floating up and out of its can!

Daily Workout.
Astronauts wear a harness to run on a treadmill in space. Without it, they would just be running in air.

Bed and Bath

You might not think about gravity very much. But it changes how astronauts live and work.

Astronauts do not sleep in beds. Instead, they strap themselves into sleeping bags on the walls! That keeps them from floating away.

There are other differences too. In space, water floats around. So people do not take showers. They just rub soap and water on their bodies. Then they sponge it off.

Going to the bathroom is also a challenge. Toilets do not have water. They use air instead. A stream of air pulls waste down the toilet.

Food and Exercise

There are no grocery stores in space. Astronauts must get their food from Earth. Supply ships deliver meals only once in a while. So the meals are made to stay fresh for a long time.

Some foods, such as eggs, are dried out. Astronauts just add water. Presto! The food is ready to eat. Other foods, such as hot dogs, are packed in special bags. The bags keep the food from spoiling.

Astronauts need more than just healthy meals. They also need plenty of exercise. Without gravity, muscles go soft. So astronauts must exercise each day.

Work and Play

Astronauts keep busy. They do science **experiments,** or tests. They ask questions. How does space affect plants and animals? What materials stay strong in space? The answers could lead to new medicines and stronger buildings.

Astronauts do other kinds of work too. They take pictures of Earth. This helps scientists learn about changes on our planet. Astronauts also make sure the ISS is working right. They fix parts when they break.

At bedtime, astronauts relax. They e-mail to their friends and families back on Earth. They read books. They watch movies together.

Making Life Better

Astronauts have exciting jobs. They get to live in space. But their work is more than just fun. Astronauts help us learn about our planet and beyond. Their work in space could make life better for people on Earth.

NASA

Ups and Downs. Two astronauts pose inside a laboratory on the ISS. The ISS labs let scientists do experiments too delicate to do in Earth's gravity.

INTERNATIONAL SPACE STATION

When it is completed, the International Space Station (ISS) will be the largest human-made object in space. Here's how it will look.

Crew return vehicle
(out of view)

Truss

European Space Agency research module

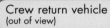

Japanese research module Kibo (Hope)

Solar-array panel

Building the Station, Piece by Piece

Building the ISS will require more than 40 trips into space and 1,500 hours of spacewalking.

Crew Return Vehicle
Astronauts need a quick way to return to Earth—just in case. NASA is designing a seven-person vehicle. A smaller Russian Soyuz craft is now on hand for the current crew.

Trusses
These are beams that support other ISS pieces.

Research Modules
Here scientists will see how chemicals, plants, and animals behave after long periods in space.

Solar-Array Panels
The ISS needs a lot of electrical power. The sun's rays are very strong in space. Giant solar panels take in these strong rays and turn their energy into electricity.

Russian Service Modul (Zvezda)
This section holds all the computers that control the space station. It also provides a living space for three astronauts.

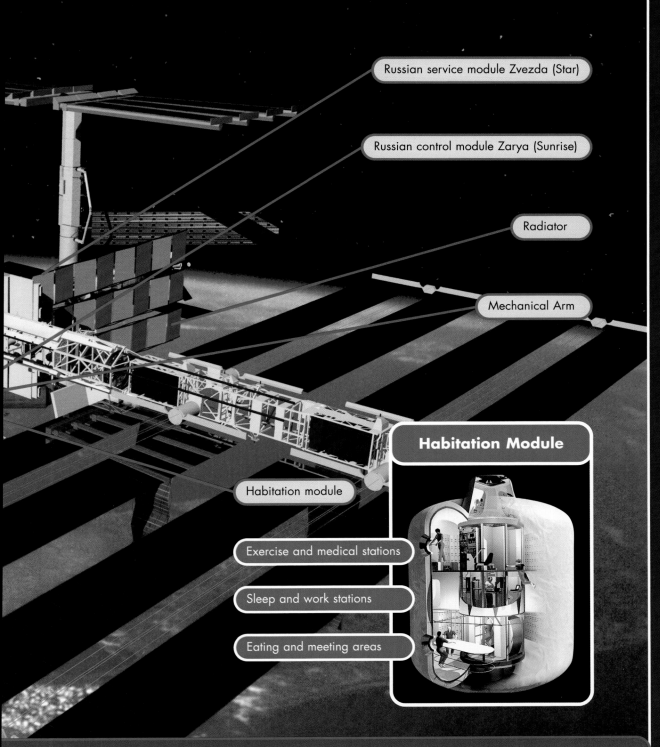

Russian service module Zvezda (Star)

Russian control module Zarya (Sunrise)

Radiator

Mechanical Arm

Habitation Module

Habitation module

Exercise and medical stations

Sleep and work stations

Eating and meeting areas

Russian Control Module (Zarya)
This module stores fuel and will provide power during early stages of ISS assembly.

Radiators
Machines that control the ISS give off lots of heat. Too much heat could start a fire. Radiators carry this heat away from the station and release it into space.

Mechanical Arms
These giant robotic arms grab modules or big equipment and move them into place, holding them while astronauts do what they need to do to assemble the station.

Habitation Module
If built, this would be home for at least six astronauts. It would include sleep stations, a kitchen area, a toilet, and a washing area.

Suited **for Spacewalking**

Look at the astronaut below. He is wearing a space suit.
It lets him work outside the International Space Station.
The space suit keeps the astronaut alive in space.

Headlights on helmet

Backpack

Pocket lined with bristles

Adult-size diapers

Tethers

Fourteen layers of material

Outer layers made of Kevlar and Teflon

NASA

Your Mission

Read the list of "unfriendly conditions" that astronauts encounter in space. Match each condition to one "space suit solution."

When you are finished, look at the letters in the answers. If they are correct, they will spell out a space word! (One letter is used twice.)

Unfriendly Conditions

1. There is no air in space for astronauts to breathe.

2. Small rocks shoot through space at thousands of miles per hour. At that speed, even a speck of dust could harm an astronaut.

3. Space temperatures soar to 250°F in the sun and plunge to minus 250°F in the shade.

4. There are no high–tech toilets to use during long spacewalks.

5. During half of all spacewalks, astronauts work in the dark.

6. In orbit, littering can be deadly. Tossed trash will travel fast enough to harm a spaceship.

7. Gravity doesn't hold things down in space. If an astronaut started to float away, he or she might drift in that direction forever.

Space Suit Solutions

E Spacewalkers tie themselves to a spacecraft with at least two safety lines.

H The outer layers of a space suit are made of supertough materials like Kevlar and Teflon.

L A space suit has a pocket with wire bristles that keep objects from dropping into space.

T Spacewalkers wear adult–size diapers under their suits.

U Fourteen layers of material keep heat from moving into or out of the suit.

S A backpack with a tank feeds air into the space suit.

T Space suits have headlights so astronauts can see in the dark and still have their hands free.

Out of

Astronauts face many challenges—from the ordinary to the extraordinary. Here are some questions and answers about what it is like to live in space.

This World!

How are astronauts chosen?

Every two years, NASA chooses new astronauts. NASA looks for people with the right skills and personality.

Astronauts do experiments. They work with computers. So they need good math and science skills.

Astronauts must also work well with others. They share the ISS with many people. There is no room for fighting on a spacecraft!

How do astronauts get water?

The water on the ISS comes from Earth. So astronauts must not waste a single drop. Once they use water, they collect it. They clean it. Then they use the water again.

In fact, astronauts reuse almost all the water they have. They collect the water from sinks and other systems on the ISS. They even collect the sweat inside their space suits!

What if an astronaut gets sick?

Many astronauts get sick during their first few days in space. Why? They are not used to floating around. Their bodies do not know which way is up.

At first, the astronauts may feel sick and confused. This feeling is called space sickness. Luckily, it goes away quickly. Astronauts often feel better after three days.

What happens if there is a fire?

Fire might be an astronaut's biggest worry. Astronauts cannot escape if the ISS catches fire. There is no place else to go!

So the ISS is made of special materials. They do not burn easily. It also has warning systems. These let astronauts know if a fire has begun. The ISS is also loaded with tools to put out fires.

Life in Space

It is time to suit up and discover what you learned about living in space.

1 What is the International Space Station (ISS)?

2 Why do things float in space?

3 How do astronauts sleep on the ISS? Why?

4 Why do astronauts reuse water?

5 How is living in space different from living on Earth?

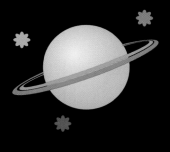